THE MID-LIFE CRISIS AWAKENING

BY

OLGA SZAKAL

Ordering Information: Quantity sales. Special discounts are available on quantity purchases by corporations, associations, and others. Orders by U.S. trade bookstores and wholesalers. Please contact OLGA SZAKAL via
https://www.themidlifecrisisbook.com

Edited and Marketed By
DreamStarters University
www.DreamStartersUniversity.com

DEDICATION

I'm grateful for my husband, Ira. Thank you so much for believing in me. You were my strength through my most difficult times! I also want to thank my four children for understanding and trusting me. You taught me how to love.

Thank you, Mike Fallat, for making my story heard!

Table of Contents

OLGA SZAKAL

A Poem By My Daughter

"DEAR MOM!
I'm proud of you."

Right now, I can say it and mean it wholeheartedly. I'm sorry it has taken me 19 years, 2 months and 23 days.

But it has never been a straight road. Our magnificent journey started when I was born.

There was a flower meadow with rivers flowing from all directions. We were close, safe and I felt planted next to you.

All of a sudden, the river began to change its course. You suddenly gave yourself out; sharing yourself with other bundles of joy.

I felt your roots reaching out to us all. You carried us 9 months, and then, the rest of our lives.

Were you well-watered? Did you get enough sun? Were you cared for?
I remember only feeling happy. I must have been really selfish. But now I think, were you?

The day came when you needed to be taken care of, that was the same day the sun moved his rays onto another field.

I totally understand why you left. You needed to breathe.

At that point in time, I took it upon myself to slice my roots and yours. I wish we grew closer instead of apart.

THE MID-LIFE CRISIS AWAKENING

A whole year went by and I missed the shade we shared underneath our family tree.

Then, you took the next big step in our relationship. You invited me home. I was far from grateful and that was bad.
You had a new sun.

This one was strange; it was warmer than the last. Once again, we parted ways, and I really missed the old sun.

You had uprooted the past; you had moved on.

Then, the years kept rolling by. Once more, we became friends. This time, our relationship was not on the basis of mother and daughter, but best friends. We still had the weeds keeping us apart; different skies, different suns too.
This meadow we once had dried up. No rivers were flowing.

Your blessings now become your only source of life, in respect to your sun. You, always being the strong one, offered an idea that would affect us all.

We moved to the desert. Right there, in that dry, barren land; **we found our spring again.**

I learned how my roots can thrive under intense pressure. You taught me how little we need to survive if we have each other.

Those suns are both okay and blessings are here to make us grateful.

Meadows can grow in the desert and rivers can travel.

Here, now 19 years, 2 months and 23 days later; I am proud of you.

...and this is why... **--Dasha**

"There comes a time when you look into the mirror and you realize that what you see is all that you will ever be. And then you accept it. Or you stop looking in mirrors..."

Tennessee Williams

PREFACE

Another Set of Eyes

Several years ago, an unexpected event occurred. It became a turning point for me. It was an event which helped me open my eyes and see that I was hiding the real "me."

Imagine a complete stranger moving into your house for a month. She begins to tell you how to dress; what not to wear. But more importantly, she asks you one profound question which absolutely changes your life forever!

This was exactly my case. This woman was able to observe my life from the outside. She also witnessed all of my daily activities, including how I interacted with my husband of 18 years (at that time) and my four children.

My utmost desire is that all women who suffer in silence and those who are unhappy with their existence could have a kind friend live with them for a month to validate them. I wish they could have a witness who could remind them that there is absolutely nothing wrong with them. They need someone who will stand next to them as a cheerleader and tell them they are not crazy to have a desire to be loved.

When my guest first arrived, she was shocked to see my big, 6,100 square foot house with six bedrooms and seven bathrooms. She called it a palace.

She was very impressed with all I had achieved in such a short period of time. She jokingly told me she would give her kidney away to have my life!

As a single mom, my guest always dreamt of having a big, beautiful family full of laughter, and a huge kitchen so she could cook all day. Yes, to a total stranger, my life was nothing short of amazing. But deep down inside, I clearly knew that my heart was slowly dying.

Within two weeks of telling me this, she looked at me with sad eyes and said, "I take it back. I don't want your life." She sounded very concerned.

Then, she asked me the one question that led to the beginning of the end of my inauthentic "feeling like a zombie" existence, which I'd lived for almost two decades. The question she asked me was my personal **wake up** call, and the beginning of an entirely new chapter of my life. For me, this ultimately meant the end of a long, toxic and unkind marriage, one which I always believed could be saved and improved.

The one question my friend asked was, *"Where is Olga?"* She said, "I see all the things you do for everybody else. You give, give and give! But, where is Olga? I don't see her. She is lost. Your job is to find her."

She challenged me with just one simple question which felt like an electric shock through my entire body!

Finally, I began to see it clearly. My life definitely looked more like a movie, but the script was not mine! I'd lost the plot somehow. I lost myself so many years ago; I stopped being me. Just like the thousands of other women moving through life without a sense of self, I had given up on my dreams, too.

On my weekly Facebook Live TV show *The Ageless Generation*™ I get similar responses from women. They often share that they are also "feeling lost." They say, "My life has not even started yet," or, "One day it all will change, but for now I'm just a mom...I have not started blooming yet..."

Recently, one guest told me off the camera, "I feel invisible and irrelevant. I just turned 50, and I already feel dead inside."

When I said "I do" to my husband, I made a serious, 100% commitment. After so many years, even though I knew my marriage was dying, I still lived in a state of total denial. I hated the word "divorce." In the comfort of my home, I even judged those who gave up on their marriages.

My self-righteous thoughts sounded like this: *I suffer, too, but I keep my marriage afloat because I said "I do!" Why can't these women do the same? I would never hurt my four kids, how dare you to hurt yours? I never give up, even though I feel dead inside. Who are you to give up on your relationships?*

Yes, I judged other women who were divorcing their

husbands without knowing their stories. I'm talking about my fellow women who had tried every option in the book from prayer to counseling, from therapy to long talks with a mentor or a pastor, from support groups to marriage classes, and finally long nights full of crying and pleading. I knew many women just like me who were begging God and the Universe to intervene while distracting themselves by having more kids, doing entirely new activities and taking on more projects and responsibilities.

Listen! Before you try to throw a "stone" at me for leaving my toxic marriage, please keep reading my story with a compassionate heart first. Or you can choose to close this book, and not read my story at all.

For those who have chosen to have a self-righteous heart, my story probably won't resonate at all. I am saying this from the standpoint of love, and that's because I've been there, too. It was very hard to stand up for my life. I was judged, condemned and even outcasted by my friends.

It is not acceptable for any human to stay in a relationship which requires him or her to deny who they are, their essence, or their identity. In my case, it was a long unhappy marriage I stayed in. I am not insinuating here that the solution to every conflict is to divorce.

I strongly believe in family as a base for a healthy society. I have remarried since, and I enjoy fully being in an effortless marriage with my present husband. He is a mature, kind and loving partner.

11

However, your own situation might be different. It could be a toxic full-time job you hate. Or a mean, controlling boss who insists on you being somebody you're not. I had to choose between the promise of "for better or for worse," and my emotional and physical survival. No one should make you choose between these things. In spite of the fact that we made a vow to keep, we have to learn how to choose ourselves first without being selfish or egotistical.

In simple terms, here's what I am saying. If you feel like you are stuck, and there is no common sense in your life, please give yourself the permission to change your environment. Please do not suffer in silence. Find a good friend, mentor or life coach, and ask for help!

I've now heard countless women's stories, and almost all of them had some kind of crisis or turning point where they were finally shaken up. For some, it was sickness, while for others it was a death of a loved one or someone in their family that woke them up. Sometimes (like in my case), it was a stranger who became a caring friend that challenged me to stop living in denial.

That person is like an angel from above that comes into your life to wake you up. They say to you, "Where are you? You matter! Your voice matters!"

We women are incredibly busy and overcommitted. We are literally hustling all the time to find our own worth through the validation of others. We keep hoping and praying that one day the abusive husband, the emotionally immature partner or ungrateful relatives will change and realize how wonderful and amazing we are. We dream that they would start appreciating us, and thank us for taking care of them. And we dream that one day everything will be like in the movie, happily ever after...

For most of us, pleasing others, which comes in the form of trying to be a perfect mom or wife, is our number one priority. This is exactly why we lose ourselves in the midst of exhausting, unfair and unreasonable goals! We need to start with an opposite approach—pleasing ourselves first!

We forget about the dreams and aspirations we used to have. Secretly, inside we know it's time to make a change. But unfortunately we either don't know how, or we simply get scared of the unknown.

Many times, we also have a feeling of enormous responsibility for everyone. The kids, the husband's mood (Is he going to be angry again? Will I upset him again?) and elderly parents distract us from changing our environment. All these duties and obligations paralyze us. Another month and another year goes by. Year in and year out, all things remain the same or get even worse.

This is exactly how I felt for many years. In the middle of hoping for a better life, I kept ignoring the truth.

When our intuition is alerting us that things in our life are not okay, we always have choices. I could have pretended like nothing was wrong, because everything that was wrong was very familiar to me. Ignoring what was wrong wasn't as scary as the alternative—doing something about it.

When my friend asked me that one, penetrating question (Where is Olga?), I started praying and meditating on that question. I had to go deeper to find my answers. I had to start meeting my own fears face-to-face, and above all I had to stop living in denial.

For me, it was crystal clear that the life I had wasn't my story. It was as though I was in the comfort of my sitting room watching a movie about another lady. To my very self, I was a total stranger.

I have met and talked to so many women who have resonated with my message. They usually tell me that they've found themselves living a life their parents or society projected onto them. Others say the life they chose to live was based on pleasing their husband, their church or whatever authority they saw as important in their lives.

When women from Generation X (like myself) were growing up, we had only one desire—to please our parents, teachers and society. We were raised to be "nice" girls. As expected, we were told that there was a certain age when we were supposed to be married, so we got married as well.

We were told to have children at a certain age, therefore, we had kids when we reached that age. Some of us were also told, "Don't have children, and place all your focus on your career," so focused on career, too!

14

Whether you are a mom, or you have never been married, the struggle is all the same. It's a question of finding your voice and deciding what you want to do with it. This will invariably translate to what you make out of your life.

I hope my book will challenge you and help you make changes in your life so that you will stand up for the things that are important to you! Yes, it's all about getting to the point where you can look in the mirror without feeling ashamed. It's time for the **REAL YOU** to have her *awakening* and become the woman you were always meant to be.

"The art and science of asking questions is the source of all knowledge."

Thomas Berger

CHAPTER 1

Unexpected Help

My entire life changed after being asked one simple question. Isn't it incredible to see how sometimes your environment can be transformed for the better if you keep seeking the answers?

You see, I was supposed to host a group of Ukrainian orphans, but it didn't work out as I had planned. I wanted to host the kids in my home, because I was considering adopting more children. A few teenagers from the Ukraine were supposed to stay with me, but at the last minute, there was a glitch with the paperwork. Instead, a social worker moved into my house for 30 days. Needless to say, I was disappointed.

In my mind, I thought this social worker was going to be a boring official. I was sure I was going to host some stiff-looking lady who was going to ask me to drive her around and shop with her all day long.

But when I met her in person, I realized she was the exact opposite of what I was expecting. She was pretty and kind. She was also funny and talented in so many ways. She played the piano and sang the Ukrainian love songs in such a beautiful way that made all of my guests cry! Right away, she took me by surprise with her level of thoughtfulness. She wanted to make a six-course dinner for my big family. She wanted us all to have a feast together to celebrate our new friendship!

The next morning, we went to the store. She looked so different from the average housewife shopping for groceries. She looked more like a Barbie doll wearing a short skirt and high heels at 7 a.m. in the morning!

Of course, the entire grocery store was disrupted. Every clerk stopped working and looked her way. One of the grocery store employees dropped all the juice bottles he was stocking as she walked past. My guest explained how in the Ukraine it is normal to be dressed up every day.

Her name was Lana, and she brought a fresh wind of energy into my life. I love calling her my angel because she rushed into my life and disrupted everything about it on every level. She called me on my BS.

She was very comfortable in her own skin. Lana radiated a pure confidence around her. She taught me that I should never give up on my dreams and aspirations either. She kept talking about her dreams and how much she would like to live in America. The freedom we take here for granted was something she strove for. She also saw the opportunity to continue her education here as a social worker. However, she eventually had to go back to the Ukraine to take care of her young daughter.

As I write today, she has gotten married and is moving to California. I'm so excited to see this next chapter unfold for her as we are meeting soon for our 5th anniversary!

Lana entered my house as a stranger who offered me so much unconditional love and validation, that when she had to go back home, she left as my best friend. I sincerely wish every woman could experience what it's like to have a friend come into their life and shake up their world with kindness and love. I opened my door to Lana with no expectations. I was vulnerable and refused to hide no more. She understood my crying heart, without any condemnation or destructive criticism.

I wish I could move in with you for 30 days. I would love to validate you and remind you that you are enough! I would love to become "Lana" for you, a supporting, encouraging and non-judging friend as she was for me!

Unfortunately, I can't do that. But you and I can connect and continue growing together via my Facebook group called The Ageless Generation with Olga Szakal. It is a safe place where you can meet other women just like you who want to have a fresh start! If you're reading this on an e-reader, computer or phone, please click here to visit and join the group!

As women, we all need each other for support. We need each other to provide honest, yet loving feedback and to challenge us. We need to be willing to become vulnerable and open and let others know when we need help.

Having someone observe all aspects of my life for a month

was like going through really deep therapy. I knew it was my chance to grow, but I had to become vulnerable first.

I was very fortunate because I couldn't hide much from Lana, even if I tried really hard. She lived with me 24/7, and she observed my entire life—the good, the bad and the ugly.

Being a coach and a mentor, the major challenge I am faced with is replicating this same type of openness and trust with my clients. Some of my beloved clients come to me as "strong women who feel lost…" If you consider yourself a strong woman as well, that is great! But please be careful with that statement. Most women including me like to use that phrase as a mask.

Please hear me out. I can't tell you how many times I have heard the following: *I feel stuck, but I am a strong woman…* and *I can't live like this anymore, but I am strong enough to make it work.*

It takes longer than 30 days to break off the mask and find the authentic woman inside. Sometimes a woman is strong indeed, but she suffers in silence, and she doesn't want to admit it. If she does, then she can't keep up with the image she has created. If she allows herself to be vulnerable, then she has to choose between staying in denial and self-isolation or allowing her deep emotional pain to surface. I am writing this with love and compassion. I care about the women I work worth and those who will come into my circle in the future.

Know that I have been in your shoes! I myself used to hide

behind the "I'm a strong woman" mask because I tried to conceal my emotional fragility from others. I was very fearful of being exposed as a weak and powerless woman. That would have been like a death sentence to my made-up image. I thought being strong was my identity, and I kept holding onto it as tight as I could...

You don't have to wait for a midlife crisis to come to your doorstep. You don't have to wait for sickness, divorce or a failed relationship. You don't have to wait for some bad event to happen in your life before you try to change. You can start changing your environment now by being willing to open up and commit yourself to self-growth and self-discovery.

FIND YOUR SPRING AGAIN

I know you want to have a happy life. That's why you're reading this book. If massive change is what you really seek, you need to get honest with yourself first. Then, if you have good friends, ask them for help, and get a loving feedback. Ask them to challenge you to become the best possible version of yourself. However, this whole process requires you to be open and vulnerable. You don't have to wait until you're in crisis mode to get help. You can start your transformation today. This book can help you take the first steps in the right direction!

"The self-image is the main key. Change the self-image and you change the personality and the behavior."

Maxwell Maltz

CHAPTER 2

Remove the Labels

I grew up in Siberia. I had a tough life in the Soviet Union—a communist country in which no freedom was allowed. I had no ability whatsoever to design my life the way I wanted it to be. Where I lived, there is almost nine months of snow per year. It was a terrible climate to live in; it was very dark and cold.

I came to America as a student with $400 to my name, and I did my best to create a different life. From the very beginning, I always hustled. I worked long hours, saved, invested in real estate and later sponsored my mom and dad to immigrate to the USA.

My father tried to save money all his life just to buy his first car. Cars were extremely expensive in the Soviet Union then, and they were considered to be a luxury set aside only for the "chosen ones." At that time only highly-ranked communists or Russians with special connections owned cars.

When my dad arrived in Seattle, he was 60 years old. As his welcome gift, we gave him his very first set of car keys. He cried like a child because he thought his dream to own a car would never come true.

Both my mom and dad loved America and the newfound freedom they had never had before. We bought them a house with a garden and a big yard. All of my parents' dreams were becoming reality here in America. It was their own dreamland. They helped us raise our kids, we did our best to support them financially for 12 years until my dad died of cancer and my mother went back to Russia.

For the last six years of my father's life, I was his main caregiver. I did a lot of driving for him, translated many things from English into Russian for him and gave him shots. I worked on getting him the best medical insurance, the best doctors, and the best medications to prolong his life. He called me his "angel," and I cried my eyes out daily until I thought I had no more tears.

You see, we were not very close when I grew up in Siberia. My dad worked 10 hours a day, often through huge snow storms. He drove huge trucks to provide for us. Although he lived a life filled with stress and anxiety, he was a kind and sweet man. However, he often had no energy left to give my brother and I the attention we desired. Ironically, I had more time with my sick dad in the last few years of his life than when he was healthy.

We had hundreds and hundreds of long appointments together: doctors, radiology, acupuncture, massage, vitamin C drips, post-surgery, recovery rooms, chemotherapy, etc. All of these things provided time for my father and I to talk and catch up. Right there, in the most unexpected of places, the sterile environments of medical offices and hospitals, we finally had each other's attention for the first time in our lives.

Suddenly, the episode turned into hours and hours of uninterrupted, precious conversations between my dad and me as a grown woman. Indeed, my soul began to heal. Times spent with dad have always been priceless. Finally I got the attention I always wanted since my early childhood, when I longed to be the typical "daddy's little girl." I'm telling this story in this book for two reasons.

First, to give you hope! Reconciliation is never too late. It is still very possible to rectify the relationship between you and your parents (or your loved ones, as the case may be). Of course, it can only occur on the grounds that both parties choose love and understanding instead of blame and accusation.

Second, if you are a caregiver, please remember to never once put yourself in second or third place. Your personal needs are really important, especially your health, your sleep, your fitness routine and the things you do that bring you joy. All these things still have to come first! Get yourself a personal coach or a mentor; you need someone who is familiar with the roles of a caregiver as well as the overwhelming responsibilities. This person is to keep tabs on you. If you can't use such services, I recommend you join an active community of online caregivers or a local support group. It's true that you are in high demand, but you must take good care of yourself first!

I have been there, so I know exactly what it feels like to have too many responsibilities and not enough time. When I was taking care of my dad, I had a full-time job that required overnight business trips, and I had bills to take care of including two mortgages. I had to drive my kids to school and activities, do the cooking, cleaning, laundry and home projects, all while volunteering at church and taking care of the everyday needs of three kids and a husband.

I work with a lot of women, and most of them are caregivers, too. They take excellent care of their elderly parents and, trust me, it becomes easy to ignore your own health. For me personally, it was extremely hard to do everything I needed to do. And, yes, I ignored my own health, ended up hospitalized and even had an open heart surgery.

Like many of you kind and loving caregivers, I had to make a lot of difficult choices daily for my sick dad and for my family. For example, sometimes I had to choose between spending time with my little kids or my sick father in the hospital. It was a constant dilemma whether or not to pay for his expensive experimental medications (for which there were chances of them not working at all).

Eventually, my dad refused to keep doing chemo, and I agreed with him; he was simply exhausted at that point. It was his choice. He lost his hair and a lot of his weight. He also lost the energy to fight. And I lost my best friend and my father.

My father went to heaven. My mother left and went to Russia to mend her broken heart after losing her husband of 46 years! I had been married for 18 years then, and I wanted my marriage to be my legacy, just like my parents who were married their whole lives. But it was at the tail end that I realized the success of a marriage is dependent on the efforts of the two parties involved. I felt like I was the only one holding up my end of the deal. My parents were gone, and my husband slept in a different bedroom for almost 2 years. I was becoming the most lonely married woman in the world...

Women often tell me they have thrown in the towel concerning their own lives. They say they've failed in life because if they had done their best, their life wouldn't have turned out the way it has. If you feel this way, then you might have too many responsibilities placed on you. It's possible that things did not work out exactly how you intended, but that doesn't make you a failure! Do you hear me? It is not your fault! Give yourself a lot of credit!

Many women of Generation X serve as caregivers for their elderly parents, as well as their own families, and they have to wear too many hats. They are the caregivers, moms, sisters, aunts, employees or business owners.

When you spread yourself thin, it's easy to lose yourself and your personal freedom. It's easy to ignore your needs. Who has time to design their life according to their dreams and values, right?

Wrong! Life might have pushed you off track. That's not your fault. The past is gone! Today is a new dawn. With you is the power to rise up, stand up for what you really want out of life, and forgive yourself for everything that has happened up to this point. I have good news to share with you. There are no authorities whose standards you have to live up to.

The only authority I have in my life comes from my faith and belief in the intelligent designer. I call him **God**.

Daily, I am reminded to have high standards for how I treat myself and other people. The intimacy that comes with my knowledge of this higher power reminds me not to judge others, and instead treat them with love, acceptance and respect. I strongly believe that we all come from the same source, and we all deserve to live a good life!

It's time, my lady! It's time to start designing your life according to your own requirements and values. It starts with being open, even if it hurts. It begins with listening to your inner voice. Your intuition is always speaking to you, even if you simply haven't had the opportunity to tune in.

I still believe that your inner voice prompted you to pick up this book. To paraphrase Oprah Winfrey, *the biggest gift you can give to yourself is to find your own true voice, and let it speak up.* If you're reading this, I don't doubt you've heard the call. So, where do you begin?

Self-image is everything, baby! It's far beyond how you think you look. It's also the sense of what you believe you deserve. Self-image is responsible for the overall quality and outcome of your life.

The choices we make every day are based on our own self-image. Subconsciously, we all project the image of ourselves onto the kind of choices we make.

If you challenge yourself to dream big, or you think lowly of yourself, like you can't do something you have always wanted to do, then either of those ways of thinking are definitely based on what you presume your abilities to be. Your self-doubts are built on your false self-image.

There are a lot of issues that can happen if your mental state is low. Self-image is your platform and your foundation. Many times, I've found that some people's foundations need to be repaired or at least dusted off.

One of the exercises I do with my mentoring clients is an exercise I call "removing the labels." Personally, when self-doubt came into my marriage, it caused me to take 99 percent of the blame when anything went wrong. It made me totally agree without doubting my ex-husband once when he said all our of problems were my fault.

Even loving parents label us, too. For example, my authoritative mother used to say to me for so many years that I was a very difficult person to get along with. Of course, her predictions that I wouldn't have any friends were very wrong.

Yet, as an obedient daughter who wanted more than anything to please my mother, I believed her!

Yes, I allowed my mom's opinion to influence me. It made a big impact. Unfortunately, I avoided making new friends during my student years.

You probably can relate to this: her voice seemed to be up there in my head, always repeating the same negative message. For too long, it served as a negative and constant reminder of how I didn't deserve to be with some people who I liked because I was the "difficult" one.

The good news is as an adult who has gone through a deep and extended self-discovery process, I was able to "remove" that particular label from my self-image. I have to say, when I removed the label, I felt redeemed and free! I felt like I had "lost" 20 pounds…20 pounds of labels which not only damaged my self-perception, but also limited me from meeting new and exciting people.

But I have to confess here, it took me way too long to do this! It would be an error for you to read this book, yet not learn from my mistake.

Today is the day! Name and write down all the lies you believe about yourself. Identify who they belong to. Keep reading; I am going to tell you exactly what to do with all those "offenders" at the end of this chapter.

I tolerated the mistreatment from my ex-husband because my self-image was tarnished by previous labels. Those labels changed my perception about my self-image.

Do you get it? Let's say another human tries to mold you into some kind of a voiceless person, and you try to oppose them. Would you agree that it is harder to stand up for your dignity if your self-image is stained by your previous authorities' labels?

When I talk about "removing the labels" with my clients, I ask them to imagine sticky notes glued to their foreheads with the written lies they have believed about themselves.

One of my very **attractive** clients told me that for many years she refused to date because she thought she was not pretty and that her face was too round. Her mom made a point to constantly tell her she needed to use a certain makeup technique to change the shape of her face. Her mother said this all the time, and my client believed it was true. You may be wondering why we allow these labels to stay. It's simply because they often come from the authority figures in our lives, those who we loved and admired.

Let me repeat it again: self-image and self-reflection are so important. They can and do influence the choices you make in life!

This is one of the reasons I created my Facebook group The Ageless Generation with Olga Szakal. Here's the link: https://www.facebook.com/groups/139344010058757/

This is a place where women can come and join us and make girlfriends, a place where you can trust other women to answer your questions honestly. I wanted to have a group where we can all feel safe with other women who are going through the same things we are experiencing.

Having this kind of support is absolutely non-negotiable. It's so important to have good friends. This is simply because when problems arise, and you want to fix them, you need people who can stand in as your support system. You want to rise up, remove labels, and work on your self-image. We all need help to see ourselves from a different perspective. However, it's important to remember this whole process starts from within.

Your homework today is to go deeper. Remember, when "self-image" comes to mind, you shouldn't view it as merely what you see in the mirror; not anymore! How do you validate yourself? Can you honestly admit that you are good enough? Think about what your true strengths are. You matter!

Honestly, you don't need anybody's compliments. You don't need any validation from outside of yourself. This is not about pride; this is about settling who you are on the inside. You have to remove the labels other people have put on you, and then go deeper.

For me, I came to the realization that many of the harmful labels I held onto in my life came from my ex-husband, and before that, they came from my mother. I had to say, "Dear ex-husband and mom, this is a lie, and it belongs to you." I had to mentally take the labels off, and give them back to them.

Next, I had to mentally go through the process of forgiving them. I had to say, "This is their lie. This belongs to them. I hold no grudge against them. My heart is light, and the lies I once believed in have been given back to their owners."

This was a key process that was incredibly important and highly relevant to my self-growth. Having a healthy self-image is not about pride; it's about respecting yourself. It's about having the courage to give all the labels you're carrying around with you back to the people who created them. Forgive people and forgive their lies, and go confidently into your future knowing that no one can hold you back.

FIND YOUR SPRING AGAIN

The first thing to look at as you begin to rise up and take control of your life is your self-image. Most likely, there are negative labels others have placed on you that you can confirm as lies. Remove those labels by identifying who gave them to you, and then give them back to that person. Forgive them, and move on while focusing on creating the beautiful life you deserve.

"Compassion isn't some kind of self-improvement project. It starts and ends with having compassion for all those unwanted parts of ourselves, all those imperfections that we don't even want to look at."

Pema Chodron

CHAPTER 3

Self-compassion

The more I work with women, the more I receive insight of the need to go deeper so we can truly know ourselves. When we are doing a lot of self-reflection and self-growth, we may begin to have some painful memories. When we start to challenge ourselves and look within, it can be very uncomfortable at first. Many of my clients share with me that when they begin to look within, they will cry for an hour or two for what feels like no reason. We as humans are wired to run away from pain. Especially you and I, women who have to be strong for so many other people in our lives. Often times, we do this because we learned many years ago to just push the pain deep inside. We hid and manipulated our own feelings for so long, that when we look within, we find our childhood wounds coming out like a storm...

This can be a scary thing to go through, because it can feel like you are going through some sort of nervous breakdown. When this sort of emotional response occurs during deep work, I always tell my clients they have reached their meltdown zone. The meltdown zone has been reached when all the pain and lies buried under the surface begin to melt away like ice cream on a hot summer day.

We have to be very careful when we go through this process. In the first phase, we're experiencing all of these deep feelings. The purpose is just to reflect in a way we never have done before and focus on self-acceptance without catering to our ego.

The ego can be your enemy. When you are growing yourself into the best person you desire to be, your ego can take over as self-pity. You might grow backwards and regress into your childhood by dwelling on unfair things you are powerless to change. The ego will start asking you questions like, "Why me?" It can put us into the situation where we become very self-centered as we start retelling the same sad stories again and again, as victims of our circumstances.

When you're just getting started, you have to focus on self-compassion instead. If your ego jumps in, then you are in danger of going in the opposite direction. Self-kindness will help you to get unstuck from the painful moments in your past. Instead of the ego question, "Why did it happen to me?" Self-compassion asks a different question. "What can I learn from the experience?"

When you're just beginning your deep self-search, it's sometimes too soon to start focusing on self-love. Your brain won't believe itself if you decide to jump from negative messages like "I ruined my life again..." to a sudden "I love myself because I am the best!" So, I strongly recommend you start with self-compassion instead.

During my midlife crisis year, as I went through the whole process of separation and actual divorce, I began looking for **one word** I could meditate on all day and night to move me in the direction I wanted to go. I tried different things. I tried self-forgiveness, and I tried self-love, but those words just didn't work for me. What I came up with was self-compassion. I realized I needed to fill my mind with kind thoughts about myself.

Number one, this helped me to forgive myself sooner. I had to admit my circumstances were not my fault. I believed I had truly done my best as a wife and mother.

Self-compassion makes me a better person, because only after I had an understanding of myself could I begin to forgive other people. Without self-compassion, you can't get to that place where you are truly kind and understanding towards others' flaws.

It is hard to forgive other people, especially those who have hurt you emotionally or even physically, without forgiving yourself first. It's the million-dollar question: how can you forgive someone who has wronged you so badly? The answer is through self-compassion.

You have the obligation of speaking kindly and softly to yourself. Start validating your own emotions and feelings.

Notice, I did not say to agree with them. Just observe and accept the way they are. Your feelings are yours, but they are not you. They come and go, and it is your job to acknowledge them without judging or getting upset with yourself.

Self-compassion in itself is about having a heart full of grace for your own soul and mind. A way to go about it is to come up with a joke you can say to yourself when you feel you're about to fall into negative thinking. Having a constant joke (or comeback) you say to yourself can prove really healthy. For instance, I say to myself when I make a mistake: "Oh, congratulations, Olga. This means you're human. You're not a robot."

I'll give you an example of a time when I used this to keep me from falling into negative thinking. I had made a small investment, and it turned out to be a bad choice to make. I lost my money. It wasn't pleasant, but I was able to look at the situation through the lens of self-compassion.

My inner voice was challenging me with harsh thoughts like, "You just lost a couple thousand dollars! What were you thinking?" But this wasn't the best way I could talk to myself, so I challenged this voice. I told myself, "Well, you lost some money. But at the same time, you were being proactive. You tried something new, and you learned a valuable lesson, so congratulations! This means you're a human. You're not a computer."

If you are kind to yourself, then it becomes easier to show

kindness to the people that surround you. Consequently, your whole life becomes better. Catch yourself whenever you dare to say something harsh to yourself.

For example, if you criticize yourself a lot and say things like "I'm so stupid," or "I can't believe I did such a stupid thing!" - this is a red flag. It is not kind of you at all to say such things. Self-doubt asks the question, "What's wrong with you?" And self-compassion asks, " What is good for you?"

This is your homework for this chapter. Get hold of all the negative things you say to yourself, write them down, and look at them. The next step is to identify where they came from.

When you begin observing your thoughts instead of juggling them, you will find out who the original source is. Could it have been your mom who said negative things to you, or did it come from a sibling? Was it a caregiver who used to call you stupid when he or she was angry and didn't know how to handle you? Whatever the source is, it is very important that you find out where your negative self-talk originates from, and then mentally give it back to those people.

FIND YOUR SPRING AGAIN

If you're just beginning to do deep work, start with self-compassion. Negative self-talk is never helpful. Realize that you are only human, and that you have always done the best you could in any given situation. Whenever you examine your life, remember this: every pain and false belief you've ever had about yourself will begin to melt away if you're willing to become vulnerable.

"Staying silent is like a slow growing cancer to the soul. There is nothing intelligent about not standing up for yourself. You may not win every battle. However, everyone will at least know what you stood for – You!"

Shannon L. Alder

CHAPTER 4

Boundaries

One of my clients owns a very successful small business, but that's not her only responsibility. She also takes care of her mom. Her mother loves being involved in her life. Her co-dependent mother still tries to parent and control her grown-up daughter. She gives her advice about how to raise her children, as well as how to run her business. This was messing with a lot of things in my client's life, especially her self-confidence.

I had to tell my client what she needed to do to fix this situation with her mother, even though I knew it was going to be painful for her. She was missing strong and well-marked boundaries. Once she created boundaries, she told me that creating them was one of the best decision she has made. As a mature adult, she now finally has the freedom to write her own life story without depending on her mother's guidance or micromanagement.

Most Generation X women are caregivers. We take care of our moms and our dads. Even if they are still in good health, we take care of them by driving them to appointments. We give them so much energy that sometimes it starts to drain us emotionally and mentally. We start treating them like they are our kids, or the opposite sometimes happens. If our parents are in a great shape, they sometimes feel the urge to continue raising us, even though we are grown up adults!

The only way you can deal with your parents in a healthy way is to have an adult-to-adult relationship with them. If you take care of your mom or your dad at this stage in life, make sure you come to the realization that they are adults, and not your little, helpless kids. Both ourselves and our parents are in a big need of being respected.

I know this probably sounds harsh or too blunt, but the reality is your parents can't parent you anymore. You have to set up boundaries. Let me show you the best way to go about doing this. It's a simple, step-by-step approach.

First, you tell your parents, "Thank you very much for raising me. You did a good job. I'm an accomplished and successful woman. I'm grateful for all you've done." Say that with compassion and empathy. Make sure that your parents feel good, and they know you do care about them. This is the beginning of setting a boundary.

Think of it like making a sandwich. You have the first piece of bread, which is the "thank you" for all they have done for you. Then you have the cheese, which is the compassion and empathy from you. The next thing to think of is the meat. This is the core of the matter. This is where you get to inform them about what your adult-to-adult relationship will have to look like. Finally, you have the last slice of bread. This signifies the things you don't like about your current relationship with them and want to improve.

Then continue with more optimism as you are really excited about the new potential of your relationship. You say, "Good news! Guess what? You don't have to worry about me any more. You are done! Your job as a parent is over!"

Then you might clarify and let them know, "I feel like you are still parenting me, and we both know that shouldn't be the case right now. I don't want you to give me advice unless I ask you for it." You have to be very clear at this point in stating what you don't want them to do.

For example, if your mom is acting as your business advisor, then you can say, "Mom, the good news is you don't have to be my business advisor anymore! You can devote the time you spend thinking about my business to paying more attention to your health. You will have more time for yourself this way, so you don't have to worry about me. Can we agree not to do this anymore unless I ask you to?"

Creating these boundaries is definitely not limited to a situation where you are caring for your aged parents. There are so many situations where you have to take a stand and create boundaries.

For instance, let's talk about a client of mine. This lady spends ample time building the online business she wants; this translates to spending endless hours on social media. Her husband also works, and when he comes home, she's usually on the computer doing Twitter and Facebook marketing.

From time to time, he speaks up, and he throws light on what she does by giving her new ideas and suggestions. But other times, he sounds like he disapproves. He doesn't see the value in the dream she's building, and he is unsupportive.

If you're in a situation like this, you can tell your husband how grateful you are that he provides for you. From there, you can then give him candid reasons why you don't think he is seeing the situation in the right light. You can tell him the specific reason why what he is doing is bothering you. You can tell him jokingly that if he keeps on giving you advice on your business strategy, you'll be forced to fire him as your business advisor.

Let him know you're not going to share any information with him about the business; not because you like to keep secrets, but because you have to protect your business in its infancy. As mothers, we protect our babies from falling down and hurting themselves. You must protect your business aspirations in the same way.

You need to be careful about letting anyone into your business circle. But it's not just your business circle you have to watch over and protect. For every aspects of a woman's life, you have to create mental circles.

For example, my mom who is in her 70s is not my

personal life advisor anymore. She's not in that circle of my life. My husband is not my business advisor either. I released him from that role. I did it in a kind and careful way. I made a joke or two about it to the point that he was laughing, and then I said, "The good news is you have more time to go and watch the Super Bowl or whatever you want. You don't have to read my blog posts anymore."

Women have a tendency to think it's either all or nothing. It's either we're very passive, or we get extremely aggressive and rude, and people take that the wrong way. These are extremes. I have a solution for this: don't be aggressive, be assertive. Assertive people know exactly what they want, and they know how to communicate their desires and wishes in a kind, but straightforward way.

Yes, I strongly agree that we need to treat people with respect! However, you must know where to draw the line. It's okay to explain to the people in your life why you're doing what you're doing and thus, lead them out of that corner of your life. Give them a word picture to help them understand why you're asking them to do what you're asking them to do.

Once again, you have homework for this chapter. You need to create your mental circles. Let's start with your business circle. If you really want this to be as real as it can be, get out a sheet of paper, and draw a circle. Decide who is allowed to be in your business circle, and who is not. If they're in this circle, write their names in it. Limit your talk about business to only this set of people.

You can't take everyone's opinion to heart. If you engage yourself in exalting someone else's opinion, one which shouldn't count, you'll end up becoming really confused and even hurt. You will also find yourself trying to meet everyone's expectations. That's not realistic. The whole process will exhaust you.

Next, let's create your personal circle. Whose names would you write in this circle? For me, I have two best girlfriends. One has such an exotic flair and an amazingly beautiful perspective of life. I also have another friend who I connected with as a mom because our kids are similar in age. These two women are the only people I talk to about my personal life. It's such a tight circle, and it's closed to anyone else. I have other girlfriends, but not all of them are in this personal circle.

You need to be extremely careful about who you put in this circle. I am lucky to have two women who are very close to my heart. It's a privilege to be there. They know if they violate my trust, they're out, and vice-versa. No gossiping is allowed. No blaming is allowed.

Next, you need to have a business mentor circle. My business mentor circle is made up of people who I look up to. Do you have mentors? Your opinion of your mentors may change as you work with them, and that's fine. It's okay to hire and fire mentors, too.

I recently fired a mentor who is a good businessman, but his values were not in line with mine. When you create your business mentor circle, keep these types of things in mind. You want to be sure that people in this circle are those who you aspire to be like, and not just people who are merely successful in general.

The last circle you need to create (if you have kids), is your parenting circle. If somebody is constantly giving you advice, but you don't like how they parent their own children, then guess what? You don't have to listen to them; don't put them in your parenting circle.

You can create as many circles as you want, but be very careful about who's in and who's out. This is the best exercise I know of for creating your boundaries. If you create these circles, and you enforce the boundaries in the ways described in this chapter, then you will inevitably experience a new-found freedom and energy you can use to improve every aspect of your life.

FIND YOUR SPRING AGAIN

Create your mental circles and boundaries. If someone tries to give you advice about business, but they aren't in your business circle, you don't have to take their advice to heart. You can "fire" them from being your business adviser. This is clearly your choice. It's "your business." It's your "business circle." Having clear boundaries allows you to have better relationships with the people in your life. It will give you more time and energy for more important things.

"Your visions will become clear only when you can look into your own heart. Who looks outside, dreams; who looks inside, awakes."

C.G. Jung

CHAPTER 5

Self-awareness

Every morning when you wake up, connect with yourself. Find a quiet spot, and make looking inward part of your everyday routine. Start your day by speaking kindly. Say a sweet hello to yourself and smile. Talk to your creator, the universe, or whatever you believe in. This will give you nice feeling of appreciation that you are a part of humanity, and you are not alone.

I do this on my pink yoga mat. I lie down and stretch. Then I listen to my inner voice. I believe God can talk to us through our intuition. We can train ourselves to recognize that voice.

Your intuition is your friend. Do you trust it? It will help and support you during the long day ahead.

You can start working on growing your own self-awareness by taking one small step every day. This is one of my favorite self-awareness exercises. Start with one question: "What am I feeling right now?" If you feel certain emotions, keep listening to find out what is generating them. I bet they are coming from some of your thoughts. Acknowledge them. You don't have to agree with your thoughts, just observe them. Just listening and not judging is a great way to validate yourself. It is a great habit to have—to be an observer of your inner monologue.

As you know, some thoughts coming to your head are not true. They are not a part of your Truth. So the more self-awareness we invite into our lives, the more clear direction we will have. What I am saying is that self-awareness requires understanding and accurately identifying emotions.

For example, if you are feeling tired in the morning, self-awareness will help you understand that you might need an extra hour of sleep, and hopefully you will choose to go to bed one hour earlier. Without acknowledging how you are really feeling and why, you might take your frustration out on your partner and even go to extreme thinking, "I hate my life. I am tired all the time... I'm so bad..."

If you've never taken time for yourself each morning, try to incorporate this new way of waking up each day. You will notice that it sets a more peaceful tone for your entire day.

I hear from women a lot that they don't know who they are anymore. They don't know what they like or want. But what if you could reintroduce you to yourself every morning? What if you could start "noticing" your feelings and your emotions more?

Obviously, self-awareness is not usually on our to-do list, but the good news is, it can be cultivated. We can develop our self-awareness by looking at the seemingly minor things in our lives first. We can develop it by being in the present; you can do something simple like eat your tasty dinner slowly while enjoying every bite.

Without self-awareness, we literally lose ourselves. We wake up, turn on autopilot and start reacting to events and other humans. The kids are too loud in the kitchen? React: raise your voice. Another driver cut you off? React: get angry. Your dentist is late again? React: be rude to his staff.

Another step towards self-awareness is simply getting to know yourself. What's your favorite thing to do in your free time? What really makes you happy? These are simple questions, but you have to completely own them. The answers to these questions are not what your children like or want to do, by the way!

For me personally, self-awareness is very important because I believed the lies. I believed that I was too opinionated, too loud and too intense. This idea came to me first from my parents, and then I heard it in my first marriage again many times.

It was the gift of self-awareness which allowed to me to say, "Okay, what am I going to do about this?" I tried for years to dial myself down, just so I could blend in. This worked for a while, but I have to tell you right now if you're reading this book: don't do it.

You will end up depressed eventually. You can do it for a

while, but after some time, you will find yourself with some kind of health issue. I hear many women complain of backaches; but that may just be a projection of pain that comes from deep within. Even though it's their heart and soul that truly ache, it expresses itself as physical pain.

Doctors are finding this to be true. Women often go to their doctor and complain that their entire body aches, but their doctor can't find anything wrong with them. They're absolutely physically healthy. It's their soul that's hurting them, because they have belittled their spirits, and they have hidden their true self for many years.

One thing I deal with as a woman is I have very severe premenstrual syndrome (PMS) every other month. This was a big problem for me because I didn't realize my mental state was being affected by my hormonal changes. I didn't have that simple awareness of what was happening inside my body. Can you imagine that so many of us would not take some time to start listening to our own body's monthly changes? Yes, this happened to me.

Often, my ex-husband held it against me. When I had days where I was too emotional, or being extremely irritable with the kids, he would say, "You see, I'm right. You're crazy. You are a bad mother! You cannot control yourself."

I remember thinking in those times, "Oh my gosh. He's right. I'm out of control right now. What is wrong with me?" You know the rest of the story, right? We blame ourselves for all problems in the marriage, lower our standards, and then we allow our own harsh, accusatory language to break us down even further.

When I invested a lot of time into developing and strengthening my self-awareness to the point that I knew when those days were coming, I was able to come to them extremely prepared. I now understand myself, and I am ready to accept my PMS struggle both emotionally and physically. I view myself from a position of grace and self-compassion. I lay low. I take a day off, and I take a lot of naps or even get a massage. On such days, I choose not to make appointments for my business. My body and my mind are asking for a day or two off.

This does not mean that I just avoid all situations and circumstances while I'm going through PMS. It has some ups as well; there are some activities, chores and errands that are well suited for those days. This is why self-awareness is so beautiful. I usually do the most unpleasant errands on those days, returning something at a store, or disputing a charge with my credit card company. I usually feel extra assertive when I have my PMS days, and I can check off all the most unpleasant items on my long to-do list that I've been putting off.

Instead of saying, "Oh my gosh, my crazy days are coming," we can be very strategic. As you can see, God gave me this extra aggressive energy, and I can use it for a good purpose. I can conquer the world with it, or I can choose to lay low. Sometimes I feel like I need to hide, and I read a book in my bedroom. I don't cook my famous organic three course dinner on those days, and my family gets a pizza delivered.

I am aware of those days as much as my kids are, and that's okay. On those days, sometimes I don't even go to the kitchen. My children know that mom's not feeling well.

Once I settled these things within me, I stopped judging myself for being "weak" or being too irritable. I was successfully able to turn that "period" into my most relaxing days with just a few hours of completing my most difficult tasks involved, too.

Before I became self-aware, I didn't allow this. I was really embarrassed about how I felt, and I was ashamed, too. But now when I know these days are coming, I prepare for them, and I plan accordingly.

Your homework for this chapter is to answer the following questions: What do you do when you feel irritable? Do you allow yourself to rest, or do you feel ashamed? Come at this from the angle of self-kindness; this is not a time to criticize yourself. This is about self-reflection only and not judgment. If you have two or three days per month that are bad for you, are your troubles caused by hormonal changes? For example, do you suddenly become exhausted, and then find you don't have the patience to do the homework with the kids?

One client of mine was becoming depressed during a very specific week of the year. This went on every single year like clockwork. She didn't know why. As we talked about this, we got to know that it was all because her dad had died during that specific week five years earlier, and she had never gone through a proper grieving process.

After she came to the realization of the real cause of her depression, she decided to see a specialist about this. The therapist walked her through the grieving process. Now she feels so much better at that particular time of year. Her better state was made possible because she was able to process what was really going on in her life. This is the power of self-awareness.

Think about one thing you struggle with, and then come at it with kindness. Don't put the blame on yourself. Choose not to think about this situation in an extreme, dramatic way. Just reflect on it, and try to uncover why it's driving you to act the way you do.

For example, if you're always irritable before dinner time, why could that possibly be happening? Is it because you didn't eat healthy snacks throughout the day and your blood sugar is extremely low? Think about what might be causing you to struggle instead of immediately judging yourself. Self-awareness is one of the greatest tools you can use to guide your life with greater clarity and ease.

FIND YOUR SPRING AGAIN

Know yourself even in the smallest ways. Take many deep breaths during the day. Observe your feelings and emotions. Sometimes, we get so busy in our daily lives that we forget to stop and view ourselves objectively. Start every morning with quiet reflection. Get to know yourself intimately, and learn to focus on your strengths, instead of your weaknesses.

"If you can see yourself doing something, you can do it. If you can't see yourself doing something, usually you can't achieve it."

Jesse Itzler

CHAPTER 6

The Power of Visualization

I love talking about my youngest daughter. She is just six. When I observe her, I see that her perspective of life is always positive and happy. In a case where she's invited to a birthday party or a sleepover, she always visualizes those future events as something very joyful. She's always excited to tell me about the happy things she is going to do later that day, the next day or the following week. I can see how her brain projects positivity outward.

All I want from you at this moment is to go back in time; reach out to that moment when you were not scared to dream. Turn your imagination on once again. This is the perfect time to do this, because you're an adult and all those authorities you had to listen to in the past are gone. You are free, and those authorities who once held up negative opinions concerning you are powerless. Your parents are not your authority anymore.

Now that you are a mature adult, this is the time to sit down and visualize exactly what you want in your life. Visualizing your own beautiful future is about creating a life plan.

Start by first describing your ideal day. Don't overcomplicate this exercise. Just write it down. Take out your fears and include only the things you want to see in there. Exercise five minutes of courage, and write down what your ideal day looks like.

After you've designed your perfect day, the next step is to describe your perfect week, month and year. The first part of your life was preparation for the second half of your life. Part two is going to be the best part. Part one featured too many people telling you what to do; you believed them and took their advice. Now you are free of their influence.

Now, it's time to drop all those toxic burdens other people placed on your shoulders. You have to agree with yourself that you are not responsible for making other people happy in part two of your life. You are only responsible for yourself and your choices, period!

While I was a student at Russia, giving up looked easier than moving on. I almost stopped studying English at one point. First, I studied like crazy every single day, and it took so much time and energy. One day, it dawned on me that I was never going to be able to use English in the Soviet Union. I didn't ever consider the idea of traveling outside of the Iron Curtain an option. I didn't see how I was ever going to be able to meet one Englishman or American to talk to them in my whole life.

Then I vividly remember meditating and praying about feeling hopeless, and then I heard my intuition telling me, "Well, at least you love Shakespeare. You can read him in his original language." This thought kept me going for a little while longer.

One night, while I was sitting in my bedroom reading Shakespeare, I closed my eyes and said to myself, "I'm going to let myself dream for five minutes like I used to when I was a little girl. What would it be like to leave the Soviet Union and speak English with other people?"

Then, I visualized myself driving a car. In my entire city, I had only seen one female driver. To have this vision of myself driving was far beyond the wildest of my dreams!

In my mind, the vision went even further. I was not only driving the car, I was also talking to somebody in Russian. Then I turned to look into the back seat, and I saw my English professor. I asked her, "Where do you want to go?"

She responded, "The place where there are hundreds of stores." She was no doubt referring to a shopping mall. The crazy thing is, about five years later, this incident really occurred. I was driving a car in Seattle and my English professor was visiting my college. Then, indeed, she asked me to take her shopping.

There is great power that comes with visualization and

dreaming. When you take a moment to pause, meditate and think about what you want in your future, your brain will give you visions of what's ahead.

I remember another time this worked for me after having a huge argument with my first husband. I remember sitting there, thinking about how I would never divorce him because of my children. I didn't want to hurt my children that way, not ever! I thought about what would happen if I stay married for life, even though he had already moved to another bedroom and ignored me for a long time. I thought for sure I might see our grandkids playing in the house with us or something like this...

While thinking about this, a different vision came. It was me sitting at a long table with all of my family, including my kids and grandkids. When I looked to my left, I saw my ex-husband. When I looked to my right, there was this elegant, good-looking guy with salt and pepper hair. He was hugging me kindly, and I felt very safe and secure around him. I remember being confused and totally not understanding what this vision was about.

Fast forward a few years, and I found myself in a very similar real situation. That elegant looking guy from the vision is now my kind and loving husband who adores my children, too! Isn't that just mind-blowing?

Our visions can definitely materialize and become as real as the air we breathe. They can turn into things you can smell and touch. Allow yourself to dream like a little girl again.

Here's your homework for this chapter. Think deeply and describe what an ideal day in your life looks like. Don't be afraid to dream big. This can be scary, but it's so worth it! Many women tell me they don't even dream anymore, so they find describing an ideal day very difficult. But this is another hurdle you have to cross. You have to break every barrier that once existed and dream! Once you've fully described and visualized what your one ideal day looks like, expand your vision from there. I think you will be surprised by the results!

FIND YOUR SPRING AGAIN

When you have started visualizing the future, the positive thoughts will definitely come. Don't be afraid of what pops into your mind. Even if what you want seems impossible, it doesn't matter. No one in your life has the authority to tell you what is or what isn't possible except you. Dare to dream big!

"I'm sure that if woman laid out the rules-requirements- early on, and let her intended know that he could either rise up to those requirements, or just move on."

Steve Harvey

CHAPTER 7

Requirements

I did work in corporate America for many years. Usually, upper management would always talk about the values. I know that the word "values" itself has become a little bit worn out, and it can sound somewhat redundant. Each time we had a new CEO, our values had to change, too. We had to learn new rules and internalize them in our work habits.

Therefore, I like to make things fresh and a little bit different. So, I always ask my clients, "What are your requirements? What are the top 2-3 rules which are most important to you personally?" You can make a list of your requirements for each different segment of your life.

For example, take a critical look at your marriage, and dare to ask yourself, "What are my requirements for the relationship I have with my significant other?" Prioritize your needs, and make a list of them. Start with your top, most important needs.

Here are my three requirements in a marriage, and it's okay for yours to be different: *I want to be cherished; I want to feel loved; I want to feel safe and secure all the time.*

As you can see, my list is not a long one. There are just three requirements for me. There are extremes to these things, and I see it in a lot of women. As women, we sometimes create a long list of too many expectations for our partner. On the opposite end of the spectrum, sometimes women do not clearly require anything at all from their significant other. They are simply short of ideas on what they want in a partner. In simple terms, they do not know what they want at all.

To give you an example, there was a situation in my current marriage. Clearly, my husband was upset about certain things, and he raised his voice. Automatically, this was a red flag for me. I didn't have to go look at all of my requirements to know this was crossing the line, and neither did he.

He raised his voice, which violated one of my requirements: **to feel safe**. This is clear, simple and fair. My man didn't have to guess why I was upset. It was clear to both of us that things went in a direction I didn't like.

Create a list of your requirements. What do you want? This is your homework for this chapter. Create a list of things you want in your marriage or romantic relationship. Be very specific; name two or three things that are extremely important to you.

What do you want from your partner as an intelligent and classy woman? This is an important thing to think about, so take your time, and really think about this. It is important that you don't fall into any of the extremes. Go for strong requirements;

do not settle for less than you deserve based on someone's inability to value you properly.

Requirements are not just important in marriages and romantic relationships. They're important for any kind of a relationship. For example, I have requirements for my girlfriends as well. My friends and I don't gossip about other people. This means that we would never be found saying anything about you behind your back; unless it's a case where we can communicate the same message directly to you, too.

If my friends gossip to me about other people, then at some point in time, it is inevitable that they will gossip about me to someone else. This is one of the things that break trust in friendships. The exact requirements I expect from them, I expect from myself, too! For example, when I talk to them about things which happened between me and my husband, I make sure I'm not gossiping. I won't say anything about my husband that I can't say to his face. This is very, very important to me.

Another requirement I have for my girlfriends is "no judgment." I have a made a promise to them never to come at them from an angle of judgment or jealousy. If they feel I am being judgmental of them, they speak up. If they don't speak up, it isn't good for my self-growth or theirs.

The final requirement I have for my girlfriends is that they be open with me. I believe in this principle because I want to live at a level where I can handle this kind of honesty. People who are your friends should talk to you with kindness, but they should still be frank with you.

This is so refreshing. I mean, we already live in a world full of lies. When you call someone your friend, you should be honest with each other. I need my friends to be open with me, so they can help me grow. The principles I have mentioned in this book are not necessarily independent of each other. All of the things we've talked about in this book work together to help you create and sustain healthy relationships.

I often see this in women who I mentor; a lot of times, they open themselves up to the wrong people. If particular people are not in your personal circle, don't open up your heart to them. If someone is in your personal circle, then it means you've already tested them. They must have already earned the right to be your close friend. You can be very open with these people about your requirements, and you can tell them explicitly when something has crossed the line for you.

I love using word pictures to describe a situation, so others can understand what I mean; I'll give another example to make myself as clear as possible.

If it's your relationship with your man we're talking about, you could say, "When you raised your voice at me, I felt like a child. I felt exactly like you were my mom screaming at me. It brought back the memories of a time when I was a little girl, and I wanted to go hide in a closet because I didn't feel safe."

When we have requirements for other people, it is also our responsibility to raise ourselves to that level as well. I require to be cherished, but if I'm disrespectful to my man, and I put him down by criticizing him, then that's not going to work out.

First, it is important that we hold ourselves to very high standards, and then we can have the confidence and integrity to require the same standards of others. Don't require things of other people that you're not willing to meet yourself. If you are in relationships with people that possess good qualities, then you will inevitably rise up to their level. You set the standard. Be the leader.

FIND YOUR SPRING AGAIN

Decide on three requirements for each type of relationship in your life: marriage or romance, friendships, work relationships and every other form of relationship that exists. Don't come at this from a demanding or a spoiled perspective; you have to be the one to set the standard. Everything you require from other people, you must be willing to give. Give people grace, respect and some breathing space. Give them time to rise; don't judge, and do not nag about it. But if they are not willing to rise to that level you've set, it's time for you to move on, and find high value people who are better matches for who you are.

"Your story is the greatest legacy that you will leave to your friends. It's the longest-lasting legacy you will leave to your heirs."

Steve Saint

Chapter 8

Build Your Legacy

When "legacy" comes to mind, it isn't merely referring to just you. It's about what will happen in the world around you when you become the person you are supposed to be.

I recently heard a definition of hell that stuck with me. I learned that hell is when we are ready to go to heaven, and God shows us the person we were intended to be on earth, but never became. That's hell!!! At that point, we arrive at the realization that we could have helped many people in life, and we could have been an amazing person, but we missed the boat.

It's true that we all have potential, but the fact remains that we won't reach it if we are not willing to grow into our highest self. Thinking about your legacy is not selfish, because it is all about the contribution you make to society.

One of our biggest human needs is to contribute. When we are not meeting this need, we might feel stuck. For some of us, this is the beginning of our midlife crisis.

One of my clients told me, *"I'm 45, and I have this mental list of things I want to do, but I've accomplished*

none of them, and half of my life is gone. *"* When you hit this point, and you're having a **midlife crisis,** you have been given an opportunity to live the second half of your life differently. Forge ahead, and let your realization be an advantage rather than living in regrets.

You don't have to wait until you're in the midst of a crisis to realize your potential. It is important that you put in every effort you can gather into growing into your highest self and building your legacy. Nobody will do it for you.

When you think of your legacy as your overall contribution to society, it can be overwhelming, because this is a huge responsibility. These thoughts could even come as sad ones if you think of this as a problem to solve rather than a way to help you move to greater heights. So, how do you build your legacy without feeling paralyzed?

You take baby steps. You take all the steps I've already covered in this book. When a midlife crisis finds its way into your life, the path forward is not easy. Taking a new direction might even make you lose some friends. You might make them upset and disappoint some family members as well.

One of my clients was a teacher for 12 years, and then she realized she could not go on teaching for another 20 years until her retirement. She realized how much of a miserable person it would make her. When she told her family she was going to make a change, her father mocked her. He said she was foolish to leave her profession. Then he mocked her by saying he had more skills at 70 years old than she had.

The beauty of being in our midlife stage is that most of us have already gotten over the care of what other people think of or have to say about us and our lives. This includes our parents and family members, too. We don't take things that other people say to heart; not anymore.

My client decided she was going to build an online business, and she didn't care what her dad had to say. When he gave her his opinion, she just thanked him, and then she moved on. As a grown woman, she stood up for her life, and she made a dramatic change. She dared to dream and imagine what might come next for her life. And she became successful!

If we allow ourselves to imagine a wonderful future for ourselves like we used to when we were little girls, then we can create a life that comes very close to that vision. What kind of legacy do you want to have? This is one of the most important questions you can ask yourself in your entire life. To design the full picture, you have to go back to the steps I've discussed in this book.

Go back to working on self-awareness. Carve out some quiet moments with yourself every morning, and get to know yourself. There's homework for you right here. You should answer this question: "What three things really excite me in life?" Write down the answers you come up with, and think about them often.

Maybe you won't find the answer right away. If you can't,

meditate on the question, and find the voice within you. At first, that voice might be almost non-existent. But regular quiet time and moments of silence will bring that voice to the surface. Then, you will get the answers you need.

Those who seek always find. If you keep knocking at the door, it will be opened. This is a promise that was given to us by our Creator. Unfortunately, as humans, we get distracted, and we give up seeking.

Don't ever give up. Instead, go backwards, and review your life. Make an inventory of all of your skills and of the things you absolutely loved to do growing up. What excited you most when you were young?

If there's something you would do for free, what would that be? For me, I love to teach and mentor. I can do this 24/7, because I'm very curious about people and their stories. I am also the happiest when I develop and have meaningful relationships with people.

Think about the things that make you happy, engage in deep reflection and build from there. What are the few things that make you happy today? If you could do anything, what would you do? What puts a smile on your face?

One of my sons, for example, loves to play the piano. Ever since he was little, he would play piano even when it was not expected of him. His piano teacher would leave after his lessons, and he would keep playing. Right now, being a teenager, he can play the piano for four hours straight. It's something he loves to do, not something he has to do.

Some of us are very lucky in that we know from the very beginning that there are certain things that are our absolute favorite. Some of us require a deeper search, and that's okay, too.

Everyone has something they can contribute to the world around them. Everyone has something they are better at than anyone else. It doesn't matter how impractical it might seem for you. Start the process of discovering it right now, and then you can take baby steps from there. Continue writing your story; it is a part of your legacy!

FIND YOUR SPRING AGAIN

Begin to search deep for the things that truly excite you in life. If you have trouble finding anything you truly enjoy, go back to when you were young. What did you love to do back then? Everyone is gifted at something. Everyone has something they can contribute to the world around them. You need to find your gifts, too.

"The oak fought the wind and was broken,
the willow bent when it must and survived."

Robert Jordan, *The Fires of Heaven*

CHAPTER 9

Thick Skin

When you go through all of the actions and steps described in this book, you'll see how attainable they are. I have given you practical examples to show you that these things are very real. They build on each other, and they help you begin to see a bigger picture. That picture is driving at one thing—your legacy!

One of the steps you need to take is to become more resilient and to grow a thick skin. You can develop it the same way you develop a muscle. I call it *"chutzpah."*

My program for entrepreneurial women is called How To Chutzpah™ for Wealth. "Chutzpah" is a Jewish word that means to be audacious and unapologetic in pursuing your dreams! It means to never be ashamed about your dreams.

In this program, I teach women to find the courage that's already within them. That brave spirit is within their heart already. They just need to claim it! It is not negotiable, my dear ageless! It is your responsibility to find that inner voice we've talked so much about in this book.

Sometimes it's very weak, and sometimes women will openly say that they don't hear the voice, and they don't feel courageous at all. This is often because we are afraid to be alone with ourselves in a quiet environment and try to listen for it.

Now, that's the homework for this chapter. First, find that voice within. You can do this by practicing having just three minutes of courage, or three minutes of "chutzpah," as I call it.

Let's say you have a task you need to get done, but it's the last thing you want to do. Instead of avoiding it, you're going to make it the very first thing you do for the day. Mark Twain once said that if the first thing you do in the morning is eat a live frog, you can have the satisfaction of knowing that's probably the worst thing that's going to happen to you for the rest of the day. So, *eat that frog first!*

If there's something really giving you concern, like you were supposed to call the credit card company weeks ago, but you still haven't done it, try this. Instead of placing your focus on how much you don't want to do it, start a timer for three minutes. Dial that number, and start talking. You've probably mentally prepared to talk to them for so long that you already know exactly what you need to say.

What I've found is it takes just three minutes of courage or less to get rid of that fear of doing something you don't want to do. When we distract ourselves, and we take a specific, courageous action, we become more resilient. Thick skin is absolutely necessary; especially if you want to be a business owner.

One of the biggest problems some women have is that they really care with all their hearts about what other people think of them. You don't have to be aggressive. You can learn how to be assertive instead.

Being assertive is a classy way of confronting people who are not living up to your requirements. Remember, we have boundaries set. Hence, if someone reacts to us in a negative way, we can say, "These people are not in my circle. Why should I care what they think?"

Some women tell me it takes them hours or more to get over it when someone treats them poorly. But we can always get better about shielding ourselves from the hurtful things other people say. The people who say or do things with no respect to how you would take it or how their actions might make you feel: good news, you can mentally remove them from your circle, or you can remind yourself they were never in it to begin with.

When you train yourself properly, you can get rid of the negative feelings brought on by other people sooner. For me it takes 2-3 minutes to forget about an offense and move on. But I have to say it took a lot of practice to train myself to do this!

For the first week you're practicing this, time yourself to be upset for 10 minutes only. When someone says something unkind, you can vent. You can even use bad words. You can get angry, but when 10 minutes are up, say, "This is their loss. They're not qualified as of today to be in my life. They're out. I'm not going to let how they treated me bother me anymore." Boom! This is thick skin. The hurtful things the person said did not get into your heart because you did not let them in. For the next week, time yourself to 5 minutes. Can you go down to 3 minutes?

A lot of women want to be more confident, but they don't know how. One of the secrets is that confident people have is "thick skin." You see, it's a lot of mental and spiritual work to examine these things. Having thick skin means not to take any rejections personally. Remember, hurt people hurt others. When we run into rudeness and selfishness, it is just a reminder to us that we are surrounded by other humans who feel insecure, hurt and unhappy.

Why would I take it personally the fact that most people are just like me, struggling to overcome their own pain and disappointment? Please reread the chapter on self-compassion. What helped me the most is the ability to feel compassion for others. As soon as I was able to give myself kindness and understanding, grace and mercy, I noticed it was so much easier to understand and forgive irritable, angry and unpleasant people.

Another benefit of having a thick skin is the ability to accept feedback. Again, of course, be wise who you ask for advice. If a person is your true friend or a mentor from your circle, then his or her feedback can be priceless.

Be able to take other people's feedback without feeling hurt. That takes a lot of self-work on pride and a big ego. Developing a thick skin will help you become a more emotionally mature adult and focus on the important things like helping others. As you spend less energy and emotion on thinking about yourself and your hurt ego, the level of stress in your life goes down, too!

This is the exercise I suggest for you to do here in this chapter. You can learn how to not react and just observe a situation. Let's say it is almost dinner time, and your husband or significant other comes home tired. He enters the kitchen and sees a big mess. You were busy with the kids all day. He is very upset about the dirty dishes in the sink, and he acts angry.

Instead of replying right away in an angry voice, you take a deep breath, and try to remove yourself from the situation mentally and physically if possible. You need to take yourself completely out of the picture; it is not about you; it is just dirty dishes. It is not a reflection on you, and it doesn't mean you are not a neat person.

What you are doing is removing your ego, and you're just observing. It is your husband or your partner's responsibility to handle his anger or frustration. If you guys have a deal where he cooks, and you do dishes, then just come back, smile and help. No argument, no hurt feelings.

Later, when you both are in a better mood, you can ask him for his kind feedback. This exercise can be used at the office, too. First, listen without interrupting. Do not allow your ego to interfere. Be positive, and don't be defensive. Be open to solutions. In the case of the dirty dishes, your kids could take on more responsibilities and and start doing the dishes. What I am teaching you here is to focus on solutions and to not take a conflict personally!

Situations like this where others get upset and frustrated with us will happen hundreds of times a year. The trick is to take a deep breath and remind yourself that on one hand, as a valuable person, you do deserve kind feedback. And on the other hand, what others think about you is not your business!

If they are in my circle, I will gladly accept feedback from someone to use to grow to my own benefit. And if they are not one of my like-minded people, I usually say my favorite mantra, "Thank you for sharing! I appreciate it," and then I move on. Their words do not stick with me. They are "just one person's opinion"...

FIND YOUR SPRING AGAIN

To grow thick skin, practice exercising three minutes of courage. You can try this out when you have to do something you really detest doing. If there's something you have to do, but don't want to do, set a timer for three minutes. Then, just commit to doing that thing until the timer goes off. Eat that frog first. To become more confident, you have to learn to let other people's judgments and critiques slide off your back more easily. To get better at this, when someone says something that bothers you, allow yourself to be angry and upset for only 10 minutes, then bring it down to 5 minutes, and then, finally, only 3 minutes. The more you do this, the better you will become at letting things go, and the more confident you will become.

"Be good to yourself, you're the only you, you'll ever get."

R.H. Sin

CHAPTER 10

Fill Up Your Cup

Visualize a beautiful, porcelain cup. This cup represents your life energy. What do you have to do to make sure this cup is overflowing throughout the day? If your cup is empty, this is a red flag. It's a wake-up call. It means you might start snapping at your kids again and even raising your voice. Start keeping a mental picture of this cup in your mind. If it's not full, slow down.

How do you do that? Yes, you are right: you start practicing a self-compassion again. You acknowledge, kindly, that you are just a human and need to have a loving self-care session. Go take a nap. Cancel that appointment. Don't do another car pool for the kids tonight. Give yourself permission to take a break, because the empty cup is your indicator of whether or not you're prepared for the day.

Here are some simple examples of "filling the cup." Drink at least eight cups of water. Have a morning routine. Most women who work with me have to develop morning and evening routines. It changes lives! It not only enriches them personally, but makes them more calm and happy.

By the way, I have a course where I teach women how to jump-start daily rituals to enhance their quality of life. It is not difficult; it takes a few weeks to develop new habits which will make you feel happier!

All of the little things you do for yourself are incredibly important, and they really serve as important contributing factors your overall happiness. To keep your cup full, you have to do at least one big act of self-kindness per day. It must be one thing you do just for you; not for your family or for your children. It can be very simple. Here's my morning routine: I wake up, I get my pink yoga mat out on the floor, and I put on some of my favorite classical music.

Then I stretch or do yoga. I show kindness to my body. I can feel the difference it makes to start my day. It's beautiful. It's a way of telling my body, "Thank you for supporting me," especially because I sit and stare at a computer all day.

When you do your morning routine, it needs to be a time set-aside just for you. If you truly don't have time to do a morning routine, then you can do something else for yourself, but it needs to be very specific. For example, every single day, I try to eat a very healthy lunch. I eat a large green salad with at least six vegetables in it. This is another way I take care of myself and fill my cup.

As a woman, you have to wear so many hats. You have to be a happy mom, wife, friend, driver, cook, co-worker, etc.

How well you wear those hats only depends on how well you're taking care of yourself.

I want to be an attractive, sexy wife for my husband every night. It's my responsibility to make sure that when my husband comes home, I look refreshed. When I take care of my body, my face, my mind and my heart daily, everybody benefits. My husband is happier, my kids love their easy-going mom, my business flourishes, and I contribute to others more.

I'm a big believer in the compounding effect. This means the small things you do really add up. The small steps you take every day such as drinking water every hour, stretching and exercising in the morning, and meeting your husband with a smile when he comes through the door make a big difference over time.

These are all tiny actions to take, but they become your good habits, and they ultimately help you to build your legacy. The results don't become obvious by doing these things for only just ten days. When you do these things consistently over a long period of time, you fill your cup, and you raise yourself to your highest.

When I wasn't taking care of myself in these ways, it was like having a powerful sports car, but trying to run it on an empty tank. I was running on empty, and I didn't check my oil.

I was younger, and I was in a great shape, but I wasn't taking care of things under the hood. Everything looked great on the outside, but I was wearing myself out. I was taking care of my dad as he battled lung cancer for eight years. Life is unfair. My dad never smoked, but he was diagnosed with lung cancer. It spread to his other organs and into his bones. I had to assume the role of the caregiver for my dad. I was also homeschooling my children, and I did that for 6 years.

I came to America with a passion and love for cultural exchange, so I also had foreign students living in my home throughout this time from all different countries. They were my responsibility, too. On top of all this, I had three rental properties with tenants which I had to manage.

It was such a blessing that I met my angel, Lana, who woke me up. Without her, I don't think I would have ever realized how much responsibility was on my plate or how much it was breaking and hurting me. I was running on autopilot. I played a superwoman role, and I tried keep up with everything. When I was feeling worn out, I denied myself a deserved break. I just thought I was a bad person for not trying hard enough...

Many women are trying to do their best, but they're still a mess just like I was. We blame ourselves for anything that's not perfect. My cup was indeed empty, and I kept on blaming myself when things weren't going well. When we're exhausted, there's no time for self-reflection or self-awareness. We barely have time to go to the bathroom, right?

If you want to be of maximum benefit to your family and friends, then you have to take care of yourself. You have to take out time to meet your own needs first before you can meet the needs of others.

The homework for this chapter is to come up with ten small things you're going to do every day to fill up your cup. Think about things like eating right, drinking water, exercising or even something as simple as listening to music you love. It doesn't matter what you choose, as long as it's a healthy activity that makes you feel good.

And if you get upset with the kids or snap again, please don't forget to give yourself permission to be human, and kindly acknowledge that you've let the contents of your cup get too low. Realize you're tired, and your love bank must be empty and in need of a refill.

FIND YOUR SPRING AGAIN

Remember to fill up your cup. If you're exhausted, and you haven't been taking care of yourself, your mood will reflect that. Then you will get upset with yourself and start talking to yourself in a harsh tone. Don't run on autopilot, or you will get into trouble. Take out time each and every single day to do kind things for yourself. I suggest you make this part of your morning routine. But if you don't have time, then do something very intentional for yourself during your day, every day, in order to take care of yourself.

"We can only be said to be alive in those moments when our hearts are conscious of our treasures."

Thornton Wilder

CHAPTER 11

Gratitude

I know you've heard so many tips, and you have a lot of to-do lists to complete to become a happy person. We hear so many messages about what we're supposed to do to be happy. But the biggest thing we can do for ourselves is practice the attitude of gratitude.

When you're going through your morning routine, say three things or the names of three people you are grateful for. Sometimes, these will be very simple things. For example, I am always thankful for my health, my children's health and for my husband. I'm also thankful for my business partners. It doesn't have to be a huge list, just be thankful.

It's a proven fact that when we practice gratitude, our blood pressure goes down. Practicing gratitude is a great way to make sure our body functions well. It's impossible to be grateful and angry at the same time. You can only choose one; choose gratitude.

It's always a good exercise to eliminate negative emotions from our bodies and minds. Practicing gratitude benefits us in so many areas of our lives. Forgiveness works together with this. You can't be grateful for someone you don't like and haven't forgiven. The Bible says to pray for your enemies. You can't pray for an enemy if you haven't forgiven them. Forgiveness and gratitude go hand-in-hand.

The number one person you have to forgive is yourself. We all make a lot of mistakes. As a mom, wife and business person, I make a lot of mistakes. But I have made the choice to be grateful for all aspects of my life experience over every other negative choice. Making mistakes is a part of what makes me human.

It is important that we appreciate life and not take anything for granted. At the end of the day, you and I want to build our legacies. We want to have a full love bank. We want to give all the love we can to ourselves, but my ultimate goal is to bring goodness to others.

If we want to receive blessings in our lives, we have to give. To receive goodness from others, we have to forgive them. They're not perfect, and neither are we.

People who are negative will always be there to bring you down. Even if they don't believe in you, you can still be thankful for these people because they are in your life for a purpose.

For example, I am thankful for a boss I used to have who did not like me. I'm grateful for her. Because of her, I quit my job, and I left corporate America. She ended up being the reason I started on a different path. I began to invest all I had in real estate (even though I didn't know very much about it back then), and I was successful with that.

When you are a beautiful, classy woman, and someone hates you, you don't have to turn around and hate them back. You can still learn from them without lowering yourself down to their level. They can serve as a valuable guide because they can show you exactly what you don't want to be like.

Yes, there may be many people out there who try to slow you down and crush your spirit, but the best revenge is just to do your best to grow into your highest self. The results you will receive from this are much more important than anything you might gain by fighting back. The good thing about situations like this is that you are presented with a chance to prove the people who doubt you wrong, not by talking, but by doing.

Now, please keep reading with rapt attention; especially if your situation is anything close to mine. When I had to put an end to my toxic relationship of 18 years, it was hard because I did not want to hurt my children. As women, our children are a part of us, a part of our body, and we don't want to hurt them.

It was hard for me to leave the relationship because of this. My daughter, who was 15 years old when I got a divorce, went through a very hard time, and felt she needed to choose between her parents. She went to live with her dad and stopped talking to me for a long time.

If she did talk to me, she would call me bad names like "monster," etc. This caused me to doubt my decision to leave.

I felt enormous guilt, even though deep down I knew I had done what I needed to do. I knew my decision was not impulsive. Clearly, I had been living somebody else's life; I knew this. I had to start over by finding myself again.

During a midlife crisis, you must be willing to accept the challenge to live your life. You are going to lose some friends along the way. My church group of women asked me to leave their Bible study because they thought I was not righteous or decent enough for them.

The people who are meant to be in your life eventually realize why you had to do what you did. I'm happy to say my daughter recently came around, and we have a healthy relationship again.

A few months ago, she gave me a poem she wrote. In the poem, which you can read at the beginning of this book, she wrote that she is proud of me. She told me she now understands why I chose to leave, and she is sorry for judging me. She told me with a smile that I am a good role model, and that every woman should hear my story. Her poem is a very beautiful poem, and it proves that the things I teach women are real and important. They are solely based on the path I've had to walk; I mean...the path from crisis and into awakening. This book is a simple blue print containing the exact steps of how to awaken...

I can't promise you will be rewarded on every step of your journey, but you can still find a way to be grateful for every moment. The people who judge you will come back if they are meant to. My own daughter judged me, but now we are best friends. If somebody told me that was going to happen, I would not have believed them, even though I knew I was on the right path. My methods really work, and I am a living proof.

I have a friend who just celebrated her 30th wedding anniversary about five years ago. It was a big celebration. All of her children and grandchildren showed up. Her husband is a very emotionally abusive and toxic individual, but she said the things she put up with over the years were a part of her legacy.

I clearly remember how bad I felt when I heard of my friend's celebration because I realized I would never get to celebrate my 30th wedding anniversary with all of my family like that. My soul cried, and my heart broke again. Yet, my intuition told me to continue being true to myself. It told me to continue believing that I'd done the right thing.

A few months ago, I found out my friend is now in my shoes. She decided to divorce her husband after 35 years of marriage because the emotional hurt turned into physical abuse. The entire situation got worse over time despite how long they were together. My friend is now alone, and she's going through the same situation I went through five years ago, where her own family is judging her and some of her friends have hinted to her that she has failed her marriage...

I want every woman reading this to understand that I am not against men. I have a huge respect for them. My dad was an amazing man. My current husband is a true gentleman. He always opens the door for me. He brings me breakfast every morning when he's not working.

I'm not in favor of divorce. My message to women is about standing up for ourselves. We have one short life.

Rise up! Stand up for your life! Find your voice!!! **Make it happen.**

Now, you may be really bothered about the fact that after mustering so much courage and walking out of abuse (or any unpalatable situation), you may be condemned even by fellow women. There's a big problem.

As women, we need to break the cycle of sabotaging ourselves and judging each other. We do nasty things to one another, and we say unkind things to each other. We must change that. You can be the one woman who takes the high road as a classy, sophisticated lady; especially if you follow the advice in this book.

This is why we talked about self-image in this book. It's important for women to find their identity and to be grateful for who they truly are deep down. No matter what you are going through in your life, I truly believe if you can find a way to approach your life with gratitude and forgiveness, you will come out stronger in the end.

FIND YOUR SPRING AGAIN

Practice gratitude and forgiveness. Yes, there are so many extremely difficult people you will come across. Even if someone in your life is extremely difficult, you can still find a way to be grateful for them. Be grateful they are showing you exactly how not to be. The attitude of gratitude is so important to help you do away with negative emotions. Holding negative emotions in your mind and body only hurts you in the end. There is no point in fighting back when someone treats you poorly. The best thing you can do to prove the people who doubt you wrong is start doing, not talking!

"When we remove ego, we're left with what is real. What replaces ego is humility and confidence. Ego is stolen. Confidence is earned. Ego is self-anointed, its swagger is artifice. One is girding yourself, the other gaslighting. It's the difference between potent and poisonous."

Ryan Holiday

CHAPTER 12

Surrender

Sometimes when we're feeling miserable it is most likely because of our poor self-image. We promise ourselves that we are going to work on being more confident, and we go to a self-help section in the book store. We get a book on self-love and we start doing daily loving affirmations. A week later, we feel nothing. Another month goes by, and we still feel like we cannot love ourselves. Many women I work with are definitely confused when it comes to loving themselves.

I get it. It happened to me personally, too. For example, I wanted to "jump up" from one stage where I was believing in lies that "I was a bad mother" all the way to "I am a great mother, and I love myself for that!"

I kept repeating positive affirmations daily. Sometimes even 5-10 times a day! I did not feel any improvement in my way of thinking. I was not ready to practice self-love at that point, and if you're like me, you may not be ready to practice it yet either. I will explain what I mean.

The lesson I have learned is that the first step to take is to practice self-kindness and self-compassion. Only then can we take baby steps towards accepting ourselves just as we are. Sometimes it's too much for us to try to love ourselves when we haven't even started working on having a simple self-respect.

Also, self-love in the early stages of massive self-growth can lead to a self-absorption, where we get preoccupied with "poor me" thoughts. The ego can start controlling our thoughts and words and cause unnecessary suffering. The ego is here to support a victim like mentality in us. Because it is easier to blame others for our pain instead of focusing on self-forgiveness and self-kindness. It's important to be careful with self-love, because it can go too far and cause more harm than good.

For example, one of my clients got divorced eight years ago, but she is still dealing with a lot of pain from that. She didn't go through a period of self-forgiveness yet. She had not forgiven her ex-husband either. She currently is with a man who she doesn't like, but she says she likes a certain convenient living arrangement. She came to me seeking the answers to why she feels so empty and unhappy. During our first session, she kept saying that she was doing a lot of self-love exercises and daily affirmations, and she was very confused why those did not help her yet...

If I were to talk with her about self-love every day, then it would not be helpful. There was too much hurt and ego in the way for any effort at self-love to be productive. The ego wants to say, "All men are bastards," but it's easy to prove that statement is not true. If you were talking to a man who just went through the same situation, he might say, "All women are b..." The ego fuels these sorts of feelings, and they aren't productive in the least.

I have to be careful with some women because if I'm not, then I can accidentally lead them into the territory of extreme thinking. I'm against that. It's very unhealthy, and that is why it is important to let go of your ego. Your ego can lead you to believe that all men are horrible, and it can make you believe you have no faults of your own. We all have faults; when we can't admit them, we are only hurting ourselves.

Self-importance can destroy you, too. It is true that you are unique. It's a given that you're already enough, but you are not more important than other people. This is a different message. ***It's self-kindness vs. self-absorption.***

There is a huge difference. When we feel sorry for ourselves, where does that come from? It comes from our belief that bad things are happening to us for no reason, and we can't do anything to change our situation. If we continue to believe this, then we are giving away our very own power.

If your aim is to build a legacy (as we discussed), you need to have a clear vision of how you want to change your life. To have it, you must surrender your ego; otherwise it will get in your way and hold you back. It will make you unkind to others, and the world will be a very unpleasant place for you.

Your goal isn't to tear anyone down in order to make yourself stand taller. Your goal is to find your own definition of success, and focus on that. Know yourself, and have the courage to go after what you want. Don't worry about money. Money will come to you when you are living the life you were designed to live. Focus first on becoming the best version of yourself that you can possibly be. Then, you will change the world around you.

Surrender your ego, and say, "Okay, some bad things may have happened, but I'm going to be the observer and not cast judgment. I'm just going to observe and ask God what I should learn from this situation." This is the only way to grow and move on from any bad situation. You have to decide to totally forgive the people involved, and start fresh in a new direction.

A lot of things have happened in your past; I understand that. We all have a past. But it's time to let it go. The things which happened in your past are not worth fighting over anymore. Instead of fighting the past, fight for a bigger cause. Surrender and learn the lesson from what happened in the past. You're missing out if you live in the past. When you stay a victim, you miss the opportunities coming in the future. You will not notice them. They might be right there in front of your nose, and you're not going to see them.

Find someone you can help; find someone who is worse

off than you. When I got divorced, I didn't have anything going for me relationship-wise, but I had money. I paid all my bills off, and I had a fat savings account. It was emotionally hard for me to be a single mom of four children, but I looked around, and I saw other single moms who didn't have any money. I chose to help them instead of spending my time focusing on how much I was hurting. Instead of being self-centered, I found somebody I could help.

In my late 30s, I had to have open-heart surgery. I always knew something was wrong with my heart, but back then, in Russia, no one had the equipment to find out what it was. When I moved to America, I was finally diagnosed, and I discovered I was born with a hole in my heart. When I found out about this, I became severely depressed.

I froze mentally for so many months. I couldn't talk. I kept thinking, "Why me?" My ego was scared. But I had an amazing friend who called me, and she asked what was going on. Sometimes, it takes just one question to wake me up, and this friend asked it.

She asked me, "Why not you?"

I told her, "I have three children. I take care of my dad who is dying, and if I go through this heart surgery, and I don't recover, who's going to take care of my family if I die?" I felt sorry for myself, and I didn't believe there could be a positive outcome.

Why not me if I was fortunate to have amazing medical

insurance? I was working in corporate America. My surgery cost almost $100,000, and insurance paid every single penny. It was my loving friend who encouraged me to stop feeling sorry and focus on the blessings I had. She told me, "Your mom will take care of your kids while you are in the hospital. You have amazing medical coverage. Everything will be taken care of. "So, why not you?" she asked again.

It was then that I realized I had to surrender. I had to give up my belief that I did not deserve what was happening to me. I had to let go and trust that everything was going to work out exactly the way it was supposed to, and it did. Not only can we surrender our ego, but also the control it comes with. We try so hard to control our big, complicated lives instead of focusing on making small daily good choices...

FIND YOUR SPRING AGAIN

It's time to surrender your ego once again. It is very dangerous to be in a state where you believe that you are more special than everyone else. You are perfect just as you are, but we are all equal. If something bad happens to you, realize it was because you have always had the strength required to get through it. The strength was only made manifest at that point. Trust that you are experiencing life as you are intended. Learn what you can from every experience that you go through. If you play the victim, you will miss out on opportunities…

"As long as I'm learning every day of my life, I will never feel old. Never. And I feel in my head and in my heart - ageless!"

Pat Mitchell

CHAPTER 13

Be Ageless

Let's stand up. Let's rebel. Hold on! I don't mean you should break the law, but you need to start questioning things. I want you to make the voice inside of you stronger and to have the courage to speak up.

At first, this is probably going to be uncomfortable. I have a client who told me, "Every time I speak up, it ends up causing a fight between my husband and I."

Sometimes, we think that when we speak up, it's going to be rewarding right away. We think people will respect and love us more because of it, but the opposite can happen. When we begin to change and speak up, people who are in our (different) circles may not necessarily know how to react.

When you start to change, people won't support you. They may take it personally. They might not like the new you or your new attitude towards life. You might experience some resistance from your husband or your boyfriend, but this means you're no longer invisible. You are standing up for what you believe. Congratulations!

My older and more mature clients have a similar concern

114

about one thing. They say after they reach a certain age, they feel invisible to our society.

When you reach a certain age, you are going to be stereotyped. You become a senior citizen in society's eyes, and they invite you to join some kind of special club like "AARP." Our society worships being thin and beautiful, young and attractive. Attractive equals young, and if you're not young, then does that means you're not attractive? No!

If you believe that age is just a number, then those barriers don't affect you. You can stand out and stand up for what you believe in regardless of your age. When I mentor women who are leaving their 40s, like Gen Xers especially, some of them share with me that they feel like their life is over.

This is why I teach women how to become part of the ageless generation. This means we're not embarrassed about our grey hair. But we're not going to give other people the satisfaction of knowing our age and labeling us because of it, either.

When you enter into a new age, refuse the label. You might still be stereotyped, but forget about what people think. Become ageless. Focus on what's important to you and keep building your legacy!

Do you want to build your own business? Focus on that. Nobody can tell you that because you are 55, you can't do it. Don't allow them. When you're in the middle of your life, and you're frustrated, unsatisfied, and working to remove the labels, society will try to label you as an elderly senior.

Don't allow anyone to wound you; don't bleed for them. Become proactive and protect yourself in advance. Become ageless and take care of yourself. Look your best. Feel your best, and do your best. Remember, do not be aggressive; being assertive is always the key.

We are becoming the ageless generation. We are changing the way people view us. It is a revolution. We will prove to society that we will not be labeled, and we will mentor the generation behind us to keep the Revolution going.

We will help those who come behind us, so they won't face the barriers we tore down. The ageless movement is about speaking up for your cause and yourself. We refuse to be forgotten!

Women sometimes tell me they feel they can't go to younger women's stores because the clothes there are the ones their daughters wear. But they aren't ready for the senior ladies' stores either because those clothes are somewhat boring. There are so many psychological obstacles like this, but we have to forcefully remove them before it's too late.

Age is just a number. We won't be labeled. We won't fake it, and our actions will not be vain. We don't have to accept being ignored. We can say, "No, thank you. I know exactly who I am by now."

Be classy. Love your body, and show your form and shape. You can do this without being too revealing. Have good taste.

I also suggest my students to go to the store and buy one classy dress or a blouse, the best quality they can afford. Hopefully it will be made out of real, organic, thick Italian cotton, or real silk. It might be more than they've ever spent on a dress or top ever in their lives. But I tell them, "May this one special purchase be a symbol of your new life!"

One of my friends is going to make a lot of money this year. She put together an online program, and it sells very well. She came back to me, and she told me, "Olga, the money is good. But the person I've become during my self-growth is the most important thing about all the transformation that's taken place in my life. My confidence, my feminine power and the freedom to be me—all that is priceless!"

When you become a classy woman, you don't go to the store and want to buy 55 different dresses anymore, even if you can afford them. You will buy one dress that will fit you like a glove and make you look sexy and attractive.

Many women want to lose weight, but they struggle to do this, and they deprive themselves. My friend recently participated in an online competition where they teach women to suppress their appetites. My message is the opposite. When you work with me, I don't want you to suppress anything. I don't want you to control anything. I want you to be yourself, and I want you to have the courage to start loving all your curves and imperfections.

Self-compassion asks, "What is good for me? What is good for my body?" Self-doubts asks, "What is wrong with me?"

I teach women that their body is their beautiful temple. I put only the best foods into my temple, because I don't want junk inside my body. I will also not put a trashy outfit on my temple. I want the outside of my temple to match the inside.

Being ageless doesn't just apply to more mature women; I've helped women in their twenties, too. It doesn't matter how old we are, we are often so busy and overwhelmed by life that we don't take the time to take care of ourselves.

Awakening can happen at any age, and when it does, we need to ask ourselves, "Who am I becoming? Do I like my life? Do I like who I am with?"

It's never too late to change the course of things. What I offer my clients is an internal makeover. I get to know your life, what kind of person you are, and we look at the choices you've made in the last five years. This requires honesty and vulnerability, but the results are worth it.

Everyone I've ever met who was going through one crisis or another always told me they were optimistic that things were going to get better. The truth is, if we don't put in the effort, sometimes things don't get better. Having a mentor who can help you improve your life is so important. If you just let your life go, you won't grow.

Here's your final assignment: have an honest conversation with yourself. If there are areas of your life you

118

need to change, don't hesitate to contact me. It doesn't matter where you are in life, it can still get better.

We are the ageless generation. We will not be stereotyped, labeled or held back. Even if you're entering your third act, it's never too late. Rise up, and become the woman you were always meant to be.

The turning point in the lives of those who succeed usually comes at the moment of some crisis, through which they are introduced to their "other selves."

Napoleon Hill

FIND YOUR SPRING AGAIN

Age is just a number. You are a part of the ageless generation. You do not have to allow society to stereotype, label or hold you back. It's never too late to make a change in your life. It's never too late to stand up against the status quo. You don't have to be silent anymore. Have the courage to go after what you want in life. I sincerely hope this book will help you do that. Finding yourself is like finding spring again. It's a feeling that never gets old. Find yourself, and then keep moving forward. It's a continuous process.

Thank you for reading my book.
Let's stay in touch.
I would love to hear from you!

Message me on

 or

@olgaszakal

Made in the USA
Las Vegas, NV
11 September 2022

55060431R00069